Durlin Family Aviation

Lawrence Durlin

ISBN: 978-0-960-01392-0

This is the story of an average American family from Colorado who were smitten with the aviation bug – the desire to fly. The time was from the Golden Age of Aviation after World War I up through World War II and beyond. As with most families in the world, WWII affected and changed everything.

The anecdotes in the story are all true. However, the author, who is the son and nephew of the main characters, may have distorted or confused some of the facts because of his own age and the time elapsed since the actual occurrence of events.

CONTENTS

Chapter 1

Albert (Bud) Wolff was the one person most responsible for getting the Durlin family interested and involved in aviation. Bud was born to Albertina and Otto Wolff in Hudson, Colorado, on February 17, 1915, and was the third of four children. Otto and Albertina had emigrated from Germany just before World War I. Otto's brother, Kurt Wolff, stayed in Germany and was the first Wolff to get in aviation. He became a renowned pilot in the Von Richthofen Flying Circus during the Great War. The Wolffs became tenant farmers near Fort Morgan, Colorado, and by 1929 had acquired their own farm near Brighton, Colorado.

When the depression hit in late 1929, Otto eventually lost the farm, and the two boys, Bud and his brother Ed, went to work to help support the family. Otto went to work in Denver as a carpenter, and Bud got a job as a house painter.

He went to the Denver Opportunity School part time for three years and eventually became an expert painter, wall paper hanger, and interior decorator – a career lasting more than 40 years.

Sometime in the late 1920s, Bud saved enough money to get some flying lessons in a Lincoln PT bi-plane powered by the famous OX5 motor.

The year 1934 was monumental in Bud's life, as he found an abandoned 1918 Harley Davidson motorcycle buried in the sand of Sand Creek, northeast of Denver. He now had his first and only transportation until 1940. He also found an airplane to purchase and build. Frank Vandersarl of the Vamp Air-Craft Company at 3001 Welton Street in Denver had the makings of a kit airplane that included one pair of uncovered spruce-framed wings, landing gear, tail assembly, uncovered metal tubular fuselage, and a four-cylinder Star automobile motor, reconditioned for aircraft use. The sum for the package was $60.00. He was allowed to pay for it in two installment payments. He would spend more than two years building the airplane before it was flyable.

This year Bud also met his one love and future wife, Margaret (Marge) Durlin. This meeting also was to influence several people in their love for aviation. Marge was the eldest of six Durlin children. The Wolff and Durlin families lived within six blocks of each other in east Denver – the Wolffs near 31st and Gilpin, and the Durlins near 29th and High Streets. When Bud and Marge started dating, he would come over to the Durlin household and found that Marge's two slightly younger brothers were both aviator fans. The three young men started a lifelong bonding around airplanes. Bud constructed his airplane in the basement of the Durlin house at 29th and

High Street between the years 1934 and 1936, with the eager help of Bob and Harry.

In the summer of 1935, they finished construction of the aircraft and hired a pilot to test fly it. They found the plane to be very underpowered and barely flyable with the Star engine. In February of 1936, they found and purchase a used 65 horsepower five-cylinder radial LeBlonde engine from Mr. Leo Schuth in Rocky Ford, Colorado. They assigned an aircraft identification mark in August of 1936 of 16475, model Wolff S-12 with 65 HP LeBlonde serial number A-21. In July 1937, Bud began attending ground school courses from Ray Wilson at Park Hill Airport at 4700 Dahlia Street in Denver. That October, he purchased an engine magneto. From October to March of 1938, he paid storage on the plane at Park Hill Airport. He started flying time at the Ray Wilson Flying School that April.

The Durlin brothers went on to pursue aviation careers in their time. Harry, the older son, soon got married in 1937 and didn't have time or money to pursue flying for a few years. Bob was two years younger than Harry and started building and flying model airplanes with Bud, while still attending junior and senior high school.

Chapter 2

During this time, Bud did keep Harry and Bob entertained with his limited flying experiences. In January 1940, Bud got his airplane registered with the CAA as an unlicensed experimental single-seat aircraft. In the certificate, his plane was described as "open cockpit, single place, monoplane. 1 8-gallon capacity gas tank, 1 2-gallon oil tank. Propeller – Hartzel, fixed-wood. Le Blonde 65 model 5D, serial #310, 65 hp." He was still taking flying lessons from Ray Wilson, owner and operator of Park Hill Airport in Denver, from 1938 until late 1940 and had logged 48 flying hours. Bud got his Civil Aeronautics Authority student pilot certificate in July 1940, his permission to solo in August, and permission to make his first cross-county flight in October. All of the above tasks were to be under the supervision of the CAA instructor Robert Cigee, #75109.

Bud's plane only had two flight instruments, an oil pressure gauge and air speed indicator. An ingenious feature Bud designed was a full wing length flap/aileron combination. At low speed (landing or taking off), he could select the flaps to be lowered, giving the aircraft more lift at lower speeds. When flaps were up, they just acted a part of the ailerons. (see Fig.1)

FIG. 1

One time, Bud related a special, beautiful flight he made over downtown Denver during a snowstorm on Christmas Day in 1940. He later admitted that was a rather foolish stunt as he experienced difficulty finding his airport in the dense winter overcast.

When he got his airplane airworthy and registered, he rented outside tie-down space at Walt Higley Airport, a dirt field that was located at 26th Avenue and Oneida Street in east Denver. The main airport office building is still there, facing 26th Avenue on the north side of the street. It functioned as a small church during the late 1940s to the '50s or '60s, and now it is a private residence.

In 1941 a new Civil Aeronautics law was passed stating that pilots may not operate unlicensed aircraft within a 30-mile radius of an airfield where commercial aviation was taking place. This meant that Higley Field and all other small airfields within a 30-mile vicinity of Stapleton Airfield could have no unlicensed aircraft flying from their premises. As Bud did not have the money to license it, he was forced to sell his plane. He happened to find a farmer in Goodland, Kansas, who had a hankering for flying and would trade him a 1930 Model A Ford straight across for the airplane. Bud thus had his first type of four-wheel transportation. Sadly, the trade-off was no more flying for a while.

Still with aviation in his blood, he started building and flying model airplanes, many of his own design. These airplanes were powered by small gasoline-powered motors and usually had a wing span of 2 to 4 feet in length. They were called "free flight" airplanes, as they were launched by hand. When the motor ran out of fuel they would glide until landing or crashing. These flights could last from several minutes to several hours, if the air conditions were right for lift. When air is very warm, rising air causes thermals which can lift airplanes up may hundreds of feet or more. One of my first memories of seeing airplanes was my privilege of retrieving landed model airplanes. These trips could vary from a hundred feet to a mile.

Chapter 3

       Harry Durlin was born in Texas in 1917. His father, Harry Sr., was a surveyor and amateur miner. The Durlin family moved to Denver in the early 1920s, and Harry Sr. was able to get employment as a surveyor and do some gold and silver prospecting in the Colorado Mountains. Young Harry spent much time in the Gore Range near Dillon, Colorado, in his teen years. He would help his dad work a small silver claim high on the top of Red Peak. Harry became very proficient with his dad's .22 rifles, occasionally getting an assortment of small game for the stew pot. Because the Durlin family was always short of funds, the game meat was often their main protein while in camp. Harry continued to hunt and shoot into the 1930s and up until WWII. This skill enabled him to become very good at aerial gunnery in high-flying years.

By the time he entered high school, he had attained the rank of Eagle Scout in the Boy Scouts of America. In high school he met his future bride, my mother. They were married in 1937, a year after they both graduated from high school. This was also the year Bud completed and soloed his airplane for the first time.

I was born in 1938, and a baby brother was born in 1940. Our four-person family now had more of a strain on finances, and so my father had to put his flying desires on hold indefinitely. Harry worked as a bank messenger until 1941, when he got a job at the new Remington Arms Company, which had built an ammunition plant on West 6th Avenue in Jefferson County (later to become the Denver Federal Center).

When World War II started in December 1941, the federal government started a program enabling men to start flying with the civilian flying programs at small airfields throughout the United States. After completing a ground school course in the program, Harry started flying lessons in May of 1941. His school was at Combs Airfield at 3500 Dahlia Street in Denver. His first 13 hours were in a 65 horsepower Aeronca Chief. The next 6.5 hours were in a J-3 Cub with the same horsepower. He soloed at 8 hours. In early 1943, Harry was finished with his civilian pilot training and applied to aviation cadet training with the U.S. Army Air Corps. Unfortunately, the military doctor said he detected a heart murmur and failed him for flight training. The military told him that he would be accepted for glider pilot training as their requirements were less stringent.

At this point, Harry was desperate to fly and fight, so he accepted an appointment for glider training. Just before reporting for duty he was told the glider school was closing, as their need for glider pilots was over. However, all these new trainees were allowed to re-apply for regular pilot training. Finally, luck was on his side, as no heart murmur was detected. He was ordered to report to Fort Stockton, Texas, in May of 1943 to pilot training as part of the class of 44-A, which would graduate in January 1944.

All the primary flight training was in the Fairchild PT-19A, which was a plywood-framed, fabric-covered, open cockpit, tandem two-place, low-wing monoplane. It was powered by a Ranger 175 horsepower liquid-cooled engine. In September 1943, after 65 hours of flying in the PT-19, the class advanced to basic flight training at Goodfellow Field in San Angelo, Texas. In basic training the aircraft was the Vultee BT-13A, a two-place, metal, low-wing monoplane with a closable glass canopy over the cockpit and powered by a Pratt & Whitney engine of 450 horsepower.

At this stage of training, pilots were introduced to the link trainer. This was a devilish invention, designed to train pilots to fly by their instruments only and with no visual aid of their surroundings. The link trainer looked like a small, one-man aircraft with a closable black hood and no windows. The pilot would climb in, close the hood and the aircraft (link trainer) would bank in any direction or any degree – determined by an outside controller seated at a console, which contained the same instruments that were on the panel in the link trainer. The link instructor would simulate many hazardous conditions for the trainee in the link cockpit. It was not uncommon for the pilot to "crash." This was an invaluable tool in teaching student pilots the importance of flying by their instruments only. Flying at night or in clouds required that a pilot have the skills learned in the link trainer. All during his career, a pilot was required to do "link time" to keep his blind flying ability sharp.

In basic training, pilots practiced formation flying, acrobatics, and night flying, along with some cross-country flights to other airfields. After 99 hours flying time in basic training and 10 hours total in the link trainer, pilots were ready to move on to single-engine or multi-engine advanced pilot training. Harry was elated that he was chosen for single-engine training – the gateway to being a fighter pilot.

His next stop was Moore Field at Mission, Texas, where he trained on the AT-6 "Texan," built by North American Aviation. This was a two-place, enclosed canopy cockpit, low-wing monoplane, with a 650 horsepower Pratt & Whitney engine. This aircraft also had retractable landing gear and a wing-mounted machine gun for aerial gunnery practice. His training consisted of more formation flying, acrobatics, cross-country night flying, and instrument flying. In two months, the cadets completed 3.5 hours of gunnery practice at Matagorda Island in the Gulf of Mexico, 71 hours total flight time, and 10 hours in the link trainer. The class of 44-A graduated on January 7, 1944, and were presented their pilot wings and their commissions as officers in the U.S. Army Air Corps with the rank of second lieutenant.

Harry was eager to be training soon as a fighter pilot, but apparently instructors through his cadet training believed he had the qualities needed to be an instructor for future pilots. He then spent one month at Randolph Field, Texas, honing his skills, and in late February was sent back to Goodfellow Field, San Angelo, Texas to relive his basic training days – only now as an instructor pilot. He instructed pilots in the BT-13 and also PT-13 and PT-17 airplanes. The latter aircraft were two-seat, open cockpit, fabric-covered airplanes powered by 220 or 300 horsepower engines. These planes were also being used as basic trainers at the time.

Harry was stationed at this field until February 1, 1945, accumulating more than 900 hours as an instructor and many hours in the link trainers. He was sent back to Moore Field for training to become an instructor in the North American P-51D Mustang. With the possibility of the invasion of Japan to end the war, more fighter pilots were needed as soon as possible.

Training was done in the AT-6 and P-40N, which was a fighter with a similar liquid-cooled engine as the P-51 engine. The P-40 had been the main fighter for the first two years of the war but was now relegated to training and familiarization with the top-line fighters, such as the P-47, P-38, and P-51. After 37 hours flight time, Harry was transferred to Mabry Field in Tallahassee, Florida, for ground school training for one month before being assigned to Page Field in Fort Myers, Florida, in June of 1945.

In early September, an imminent hurricane caused all pilots and aircraft to go north to the Army air field at Sarasota, Florida. After about 105 hours of flying time between then and the first week of November 1945, flying operations were shut down in Sarasota. The war had ended in September and the need for new fighters was over.

Chapter 4

Many pilots were ready to end their military flying careers, but Harry would take any assignment to stay in the Army and keep flying. The result was an assignment in November 1945 to report to Marshall Field, Fort Riley, Kansas. This was the home of the 1st Cavalry Division, and 1st Lt. Harry Durlin was assigned the task of flying the Stinson L-5 liaison plane. This was a 150 horsepower, fabric-covered, high-winged, two-seater for flying artillery officers around occasionally and for reconnaissance duties in aiding army ground troops. Occasionally, he was able to fly an AT-6 to keep up his instrument and acrobatic skills. He was also able to fly home to Denver and see his wife and son (me) on a Christmas holiday.

In November 1945, Harry was to fly to Fort Worth, Texas, by way of several air bases en route to Texas. The L-5 aircraft only had fuel capacity for a few hundred miles, which made it mandatory to fuel up at three air bases on the trip. As was the frequent habit, a young enlisted man was able to hitch a ride in the rear seat to their Fort Worth destination. As their first leg of the trip was just less than 150 miles to Coffeyville, Kansas, they departed late in the day. Unfortunately, after dark they ran into several thunderstorms. In trying to circumvent the storms, they were running out of fuel.

Harry said to the young enlisted man, "Son, I am going to try to land this thing somewhere, but if you would rather use your parachute and jump, I wouldn't blame you."

His wide-eyed and meek answer was, "No Sir, I will stick with you!"

My dad was able to land in a small, muddy onion patch. No damage was done to the plane. The next morning Harry was able to get official permission to get gas and take off from an adjacent dirt road and continue on their trip. This was the only forced landing Harry ever had to make in 10 years of flying time from 1942 through 1952 – a total of more than 2,500 hours.

In May 1946, Harry was transferred to Giebelstadt, Germany, for a refresher course in flying P-51s by way of some time in AT-6s and P-51s. After 38 hours flying time in October 1947, Harry was transferred to the 308th fighter squadron of Kitzingen, Germany, for duty in occupation forces at the end of WWII. In February and March, a few new Lockheed P-80 fighter jets were sent to their base for the pilots to try out. Harry had two one-hour flights in this new plane. All pilots agreed that the "80," with its hydraulic-boosted flight controls, had a tendency to over control, but it was faster and still very maneuverable.

In June 1947 after 136 hours flying time, Harry was transferred back to the United States to attend jet transition school at Williams Air Base in Chandler, Arizona. That November, after 39 hours in P-80 and AT-6 aircraft, Harry was assigned to the 1st fighter group, 71st Fighter Squadron at March Field, Riverside, California.

In early 1948 the United States Air Force was formed as a separate branch of the armed forces. The days of the Army Air Forces were over. As of this date, the designation for fighter planes was changed from "P" for pursuit to "F" for fighter. For example – P-51 was now F-51 and P-80 was now the F-80.

While Harry was with the 71st Squadron, there were several special assignments. The first was three-day maneuvers in March 1948 with combined air and ground forces on opposing sides to simulate winter combat operations. The 71st was stationed at Peterson Field in Colorado Springs, Colorado, and they were to attack winter ground troops in the area of Camp Hale in the Rocky Mountains. Harry and his wingman came up a valley about 100 feet above the snow-covered ground. They caught a couple of snow-treaded personnel carriers completely by surprise. With jet aircraft you don't hear their engines until they are overhead. The gun cameras of the F-80s showed the arms, legs, and skis jumping into the snow as they roared overhead. The other team lost that round.

In May 1948, part of the 94th and 71st squadrons were sent to Spokane, Washington, for eight days. Actually, the aircraft just stopped at Spokane Airfield to refuel and all went to Ladd Air Force Base in Alaska. This was a secretive, classified mission to test the still-new jet aircraft under extreme cold weather conditions. This mission did not show up in pilots' log books. However, some home photos did show airplanes and pilots in an obvious Alaskan location.

In September 1948, the entire 1st fighter group went to Brookley Field in Mobile, Alabama, for joint service maneuvers with the Air Force, Army, and Navy units for 30 days in exercises called Operations "Combine III."

In early 1948 Harry and his squadron leader, Colonel Petit, were privileged to fly factory fresh F-80Bs from the Lockheed plants at Burbank, California, to March Field near Riverside, California. Their aircraft were identified as FT712 and FT713. In 1990 I was visiting Smithsonian Air and Space museum in Washington D.C. and was viewing the first P-80 prototype. On display on the wall behind the airplane was a large oil painting depicting a P-80 in flight. The plane was clearly identifiable as number FT-713 of 71st Squadron, which was Colonel Petit's airplane. Small world!

In mid-December of 1948, Harry and four other pilots were chosen as replacement pilots to the 31st fighter group, 22nd squadron, in Furstenfeldbruck Air Base in Germany. There was a necessary build-up of U.S. air strength in Germany to address the threat of Cold War escalation. Harry had time for Christmas in Denver with the family before departing for Germany in January 1948.

Duties for the 22nd fighter squadron in Furstenfeldbruck were mostly patrolling the East and West German borders opposite Russian air forces in typical Cold

War standoff. By late summer 1949, tensions were somewhat eased after Russia lifted its blockade of West Berlin. Routine flying for the 31st group was now enabling operations for some cross-country flying which led to an interesting adventure. The following is a narrative from Harry as related in a letter to his wife back in Denver:

Sat Aug 27 1949
6:30 P M

I've just gotten back XXXX from somewhere. I had to spend a couple of days in Rome, - XXXX but though I don't much care for the place-I felt fortunate to be there. The clipping I cut out of the Stars and Stripes explains why I was there, I reckon.

It was quite an ordeal,- that flight. XXXXXXXXXXXXX Gleason, Maj Harris. Wallace and I went down to Rome Wed. morning and spent the day, planning to come back at night to get our night time in. After spending a nice day in town, we went out to the field in the evening to leap off for home. After a good spaggitti dinner at the Airline Terminal, We took off just about dark. I was last off and had a little trouble getting my cockpit lights on while taxing out, which delayed me taking offabout one minute. Due to the haze and darkness I

couldn't see the lights of the other three
ships and didn't get joined up with them.
(Luckily I guess). George Gleason set his
course and called me as he was over several
visible check points the first 50 miles and
I was about 5 miles behindthe flight at each
one. Before I could catch them however he
ran into instrument conditions, so naturally
we planned no further attempt for me to join them.
He knew I'd be OK returning by myself, so I
came individually. The stuff got worse and
we were unable to top it at 27,000 ft. by
the time we got to the Alps. I finally get
to 35.000 ft. and still was in it most of
the time so I didn't try to go any
higher. I was somewhere within 5 miles of
his he and his wingmen all the way and we
talked back and forth over the radio all the
way. Anyhoo.- he started his let downbeyond
the Brenner Pass,- Approximately over
Innsbruck, and was most of the way down
through the solid overcast which was about
22,000 ft. thick when he apparently flew
right into a thunder storm. I was just to
the point to start start my let down by then
and was just starting to when he called me
and said how bad it was and if I still had

my altitude he'd advise me to turn around
and make it back to Rome. From the trouble I
could hear they were having , - it sounded
like a good idea to me. I was still in my
turn when I heard him call first one of his
wingmen and then the other to ask them where
they were and if they were OK. He called
each 3 times and no answer. I answered him
so he'd know he was transmitting OK. He came
back and said he was afraid he'd lost ~~both~~
his wingmen. A bolt of lightning (which was
continuous and every where) had hit his ship
and blinded both his wingmen who peeled off
in opposite directions. After several
minutes I heard Maj.Harris answer him but
his transmission was pretty shaky and weak.
About all I could make out was that he was
down to 4500 Ft. and ░░░░░░░░░░░ "thought
he was OK but was still blinded". Apparently
he might have been inverted because a matter
of seconds later he went in, - as straight
down as an airplane can so making a hole
only 9 ft in diameter. At any rate I thought
for sure that Wally had had it. But he had
bailed out and except for his face looking
like he has been shot with a shotgun, from
hitting the rain at such a high speed and a

18

sprained hip he is all OK. I didn't know for
sure till I got back ▒▒▒▒ here how it was.

Anyway to keep from making this too
long I'll just say that I had some troubles
of my own getting the 400 miles back to
Rome. I held 35,000 ft on the way back as
long as I could though I was still on
instruments. And believe me,- that is a
handful to try to fly the guages the way
that thing handles at that altitude at night
and through the tops of ▒▒▒▒▒▒▒▒▒▒▒▒
thunderstroms where the turbulence turns you
every way but loose. The lightening and
static was so bad that I turned every light
I could find on in the cockpit and lowered
the seat clear down and didn't dare look
out. the canopy was glowing like a neon
light with ST. ElmosFire. But the worst
feature was that it cut my radio compass
completely out and it wouldn't home on the
Rome Range at all. I had visions of winding
up in the cold Meditteranean and no life
vest. Anyhoo, the conditions had gotten
worse all the way back to Rome and I finally
had to start ▒▒▒▒▒▒ letting down as I was
about out of oxygen and getting numb from

the cold. I later fond the knuckle on one of
my fingers frostbitten,- but not bad,- just
the tip. Anyway just as I reached 14,000 ft.
and was figuring I was surely past Rome I
suddenly popped out of the face of the
clouds and the old "town pointer" (radio
compass) swung right around to 0 as the
static stopped instantly as I came out of
the cloud. ~~IXXIXEXYXIXHXX~~ and as I raised up
and peered out there was a big dull glow
directly ahead about 25 mi- Rome! Golly,
did it look welcome! I had to circle for 15
min. to let some of the ice melt off the
canopy and finally came in anyway, slipping
all the way down to the end of ~~XXHXXHYXXYX~~
the runway so I could look out of the side
as the front glass was still iced up a half
inch thick both inside and outside. I had to
stand up and look over the top of it to taxi
in.

-Amen*

Golly, I'm sorry I've written such a
book about the flight. Guess I need
something out of the ordinary like that to
write a long letter. Oh yes - one more
~~littel~~ little thing about it and then I'll shush

about it. When I got back there that night,
- I had no money with me, no cigarettes, or
no nothing. There's no place to stay on the
field either, but I was glad enough to be
there that I didn't care if I slept in my
airplane. (Incidentally the weather soaked
in right down to the ground 20 min after I
landed). Anyway I ran into a Master Sgt.from
Trieste who was waiting for a M.A.T.S. ship
to come in as he XXXXXXXX was going back
to the States on an emergency furlough. Well
he insisted he was going to loan me $20.00
so I could eat and sleep, etc. for however
many days I would be there. I told him I
didn't know how I could get it back to him
but he didn't care. Suddenly I remembered I
still had a blank check form in my bill fold
I'd been carring since I was home. So I
wrote him a check and dated it Sept. 1st,-
so then I felt XXX better about accepting
it.

Taken from letter written by

XXXXXXXXXXXXXXXXXXXXXXX

LT. HARRY L. DURLIN Jr.

GERMANY.

Throughout 1949, the 22nd squadron visited England, Sweden, and Greece and made several trips to Malta and Rome. That year several instrument landing approaches were made via GCA (ground control approaches) where radar operators on the ground were able to talk down pilots to within a few feet of the runway without any visual contact of the pilots with the ground.

In February 1950, there was an overall economy cut in armed forces spending, and the Air Force made cutbacks in personnel. My father, Harry Durlin, was deemed over age for his rank of first lieutenant and was rendered inactive immediately. His total flying time with the 22nd squadron was 171 hours. My mother and I were military dependents in Germany at that time, so we all returned to the United States together. My father officially exited active duty at Lowry Air Force Base in Denver on March 31, 1950, after being able to accumulate his flight time for March in B-25 and C-47 aircraft.

Harry was determined to keep flying at age 32 and thus entered the Colorado Air National Guard at Buckley Field, Denver, Colorado in October of 1950. He was assigned to the 120th fighter squadron to fly the P-51D, his favorite propeller-driven airplane. Before he could get back in his favorite fighter, he had to accomplish 20 hours of combined T-6, C-47, and link trainer time over three months.

Finally in January of 1951, he was back in the air until April 1, 1951, when he was ordered back to active duty by special orders to attend F-86 fighter school at Nellis Air Force Base in Las Vegas, Nevada. When Harry was called back to active duty, he was promoted to the rank of captain. Harry continued to fly P-51s until the start of school in August 1951. The Nellis training consisted of training in high and low altitude bombing, high and low altitude strafing, rocket firing, and much air-to-air combat. His overall score for all of this training was 89 percent.

After 106 hours in the F-86, Harry returned to Buckley Field and the 120th squadron until November 1951, when the squadron was moved to Clovis Air Force Base, New Mexico, where 70 more hours were spent in the P-51 while waiting for further assignment.

In May, he was sent to Tsuiki Air Base, Japan, for a 44-hour course in maintenance of the F-86E, which was replacing the F-86A in combat operations. By May 15, 1952, he arrived at Air Base K-13, Suwon, Korea – the home of the 51st Fighter Group, commanded by Colonel "Gabby" Gabreski, an ace of World War II and Korea. Harry was assigned to the 25th Fighter Interceptor Squadron and was fortunate to room with Major Walt Williams, a pilot and friend from the 120th Fighter Squadron at Buckley Field in Denver. From mid-May through August, there was intense air activity in "MiG Alley" over North Korea for all United Nations forces facing the Communist air forces of North Korea, China, and the U.S.S.R.

In addition to being the squadron gunnery officer, Harry was a flight commander of 10 pilots for each flight. (Five second lieutenants, two first lieutenants, and two majors). Being the flight commander meant scheduling flights and keeping track of all the pilots' flight equipment. But being the flight leader, he also had the first opportunity to shoot at the enemy.

The first two weeks of August saw heavy enemy air action for the 51st Fighter Group. On the 4th and 5th of

August, Harry had two days of intense dogfighting. The following letter to me back in Colorado describes the action:

"The 4th of August I was heading the 2nd element of Captain Henderson's flight (he has 2 ½ MiGs to his credit) and were patrolling up the Yalu River. An element of MiGs passed below going in the opposite direction on the far side of him from me. He racked it around and went down on them, and just as he did, I saw this second element of theirs, who were above, come down behind him – shooting as they came. I was in a turn behind him, already, and I called him that he was being fired on and all I had to do was pull it in a little, and I was behind the leader of the second element who was pumping away at him. They have one 37mm cannon and two 23mm cannons, and he was really on them, blasting away as he came down in his turn. I had no trouble lining up behind him – I don't think he knew I was back there – and I really clobbered him good for a few seconds. He snapped underneath – and I thought I had him – as I had some visible hits, but he pulled it thru and split-essed down, pulling away across the river to Manchuria. We were at 38,000 feet, so I couldn't begin to stay with him. Anyway, it gave me a lot of satisfaction to clobber one who was shooting one of ours. He was really leaving some 'puffs' in the sky with his cannons, and I don't think he knew I was back there until he got hit.* Then the next day, I was with Henderson again, and we got into it with six of them, but never did get a good shot, as we'd chase the two down at our altitude, and there were four more who would keep 'yo-yoing' us from above. They came down thru us firing – head on – once, but it sure didn't worry us any, as they couldn't hope to do any good that way. We went around with them for about 10 solid minutes, which is a long time in these deals. Anyway, I sure have a lot of respect for that MiG – especially at altitude.

The way they would come down us – and then pull back up to 42,000 feet above us, really amazes me. I'll no doubt go for about 25 'milk runs' without seeing anything now."

*For his action on August 4, Harry was awarded a probable, as the MiG he shot was trailing smoke and going down – but made across the Yalu River into Manchuria, which was off limits to all U.N. forces.

Harry did only have 24 more combat missions before being grounded for medical reasons on September 17, 1952. Lt. Durlin was diagnosed with an unknown ailment and was unable to perform any duties. He was ill enough to be shipped to a hospital in Japan by October 1. Harry was then transferred to a military hospital in San Francisco, where it was thought that he had pneumonia and a possible nervous affliction. It was 15 more days before he was deemed well enough to transfer him to Fitzsimons Army Hospital in Denver. The doctors were then able to correctly diagnose Harry's condition as lung cancer. He succumbed to this disease on January 8, 1953. He had a rewarding, but short, flying career with a total of 2,547 hours, 724 of them in jet aircraft.

Chapter 5

Robert C. (Bob) Durlin was born in Denver in 1921. He was just two years younger than Harry, and they were very close during the years up through their late teens. Bob graduated from Manual High School in 1939 and went to San Angelo Junior College in San Angelo, Texas. He was able to work for his Uncle Bob Kenney, who owned a local service station. He also lived with his aunt and uncle while attending college.

In 1941, when it looked like we would be in war soon, Bob applied and was accepted in the Army Aviation Cadet Training program. He went through primary and basic training at Randolph and Kelly Fields. He then graduated from advanced training at Foster Field in the class of 42F with his new wings and second lieutenant commission. He was soon assigned to 353rd fighter group, 352nd squadron flying the P-47D aircraft. The group was in New Jersey until May 1943, when they shipped to England to be based at an airfield at Bodney, Norfolk. The group started flying missions over occupied France in late June. Bob was soon made a flight leader and promoted to the rank of captain. Through July and August, the squadrons of the group were flying combat patrol missions, looking for enemy fighters, or they were escorting bombers on missions into central France.

On September 15, Bob was leading an element of four aircraft back from a bomber escort mission to targets near Paris. As the official mission report stated: "As the squadron returned from the mission the appalling weather and increasing darkness resulted in the loss of two aircraft and one pilot. Capt. Robert C. Durlin, a senior squadron pilot and "A" flight leader, flying SX-A (a/c 42-8420) and 2nd Lt. Walter Donovan flying SX-W (a/c 42-8494) got into difficulties and were forced to bail out."

Durlin described what happened in the Missing Air Crew Report (No. 625):

"I was departing from the French Coast after an escort mission, leading a flight of four ships. Upon attempting to descend through an overcast with the flight, I discovered part of my flight instruments were inoperative (flight indicator needle). I orbited 360 degrees to port with my wingman, going through a hole in the overcast a short distance from the French Coast. The second element lost me in the turn and evidently continued its course above the overcast.

Visibility below the overcast was extremely poor, so I continued on (330 degrees) on what I considered the correct compass course. Shortly after I encountered what I thought was the English Coast, but which turned out to be the French Coast, as an intense anti-aircraft barrage was encountered. The compass was swinging consistently through a 180-degree arc. Not trusting the compass, I called several times for an emergency homing on Channel 'D,' but received no reply.

My wingman, Donovan, called and said that he had to bail out near an island off the French coast. I switched to emergency IFF and went to Channel 'B' and gave a mayday for Donovan but was unable to remain in the vicinity due to the intense flak barrage from a nearby island.

I climbed back into the overcast through a small hole, continuing my call for homing on 'D' channel. Due to the inaccuracy of my compass, I was unable to follow the vector given by homer. I continued on as best as I could figure on a northwest heading to England, darkness having already descended. My fuel gave out a short time later, and I gave a mayday on channel 'B' and switched the IFF to emergency.

I rolled the slip over and bailed out at about 6,000 feet, at about 20.30 hours. When I thought I was free of the ship, I became aware of a fluttering sound overhead. Then I noticed my chute was already partially opened, without my having pulled the ripcord. I also saw the shrouds were tangled and the canopy was torn. I struggled with the shroud lines, attempting to untangle them. This opened the chute about halfway. I continued to work on the shroud lines until I struck the ground and lost consciousness. I regained consciousness about an hour and a half later and was found by searchers about one and a half hours after that."

His airplane hit the ground at a steep angle and was seen by a young farm boy on the Week Orchard farm near Bude, Cornwall. Amazingly in 2012, an archaeological team that deals in World War II artifacts was contacted by this gentleman of 70-plus years old and was directed where to dig for aircraft remnants in the farm field. A large backhoe located some remains under 6-7 feet of soft farm soil after several hours of digging. The only very recognizable piece of the wreckage was the fairly intact Pratt & Whitney R-2800 double wasp radial engine. I saw pictures of the excavated engine on the internet, but don't know its ultimate destination. – Author

Bob had pneumonia, which was addressed first, so his other injuries were not dealt with for several hours. His wingman, second lieutenant Donovan, was never found.

In the hospital, it was discovered that Bob had broken both ankles and several vertebrae. After a few weeks in the hospital, Bob was sent home in his partial body cast on the Queen Mary. Bob then recuperated in a military hospital in Texas. During early 1944, he was able to visit with Harry, who had just been stationed as an instructor in basic training at San Angelo. Bob was then walking but still had a cast, which he soon traded for a back brace and would wear until 1950. However, Bob was deemed physically fit enough to fly and would be assigned to Peterson Field, Colorado Springs, Colorado, until the end of the war. He had an enviable duty of test flying aircraft after they had been repaired, so that they might be returned to combat duty.

When the war ended, Bob married fiancée Ruth McDowell of Denver. After their wedding (Bob still wore his military uniform for the ceremony), he got out of the service in 1946 and was soon hired as a copilot for United Airlines, flying

DC-3s. By 1951 Bob was flying DC-4s and DC-6s and was promoted to first pilot. In 1952 he settled in a house in south Denver and was the father of three boys, ages 18 months through six years old. He was a captain for United Airlines flying D-6Bs. United was contracted to supply personnel and supplies to the Korean War theater as far as Japan via San Francisco, Honolulu, Wake Island, and Tokyo. Bob would fly four days and be home four days, depending on weather. Often they would layover on Wake Island and be able to go swimming in the Pacific Ocean.

In November 1952, at home, Bob mentioned the undertow was strong in the ocean. Bob was a good swimmer, but for an unknown reason – not good enough. On New Year's Day, 1953, Bob went swimming and he drowned in the undertow.

The two eldest Durlin brothers, ages 36 and 34, died within 8 days of each other. The brothers were interred in back-to-back graves at Fort Logan Military Cemetery in Denver. As Harry was still on active duty at the time of his death, and because he had been a member of the 120th Fighter Squadron at Buckley Field, he had a touching service at graveside, including a "missing" man flyover of 120th Fighter Squadron P-51s, a 21-gun salute, and taps.

Chapter 6

Bud was also mechanically inclined and interested in learning aircraft mechanics. He attended Denver Opportunity School in 1940 for several months. In February of 1941 he was hired by Denver Municipal Airport (Stapleton Field) as an airplane and engine mechanic under the supervision of a Civil Aviation Authority-certified mechanic. Bud worked at Denver Municipal Airport until late 1941. When he got his draft notice by Uncle Sam in July 1942, he went to the enlistment office with the hope of becoming a liaison pilot – that is, a pilot of small airplanes for various military duties requiring small airplane pilot skills. The army, however, had other plans and sent Bud to school for electronic training for gunsights and gun turrets. Because his duties would probably be stateside during the war, Bud and Marge finally decided to get married. Bud spent the next three years stationed at Casper Army Air Base in Wyoming, Hill AFB in Ogden, Utah, and finally, George

AFB in Victorville, California. By then, he was an instructor in bomber gun turrets and held a rank of technical sergeant.

In early 1945, Bud and several other technicians were sent to Mountain Home, Idaho, on a secret classified assignment. They were to modify five B-29 bombers. Mostly they removed many of the machine guns and other heavy equipment. Only after the war did the crew find out that the B-29s were being prepared for the atomic bomb missions in August 1945.

When the war was over, Bud returned to civilian life and resumed his career as a house painter, but this time he went into business for himself with one or two assistants. Still not having enough funds to buy another airplane, he continued constructing and flying model airplanes. Newly arrived on the postwar scene was the start of "control-line flying." Airplanes were flown in a circle, connected to the operator by two lines and a handle. The handle controlled the raising and lowering of the tail control surfaces, thus enabling the operator to "fly the airplane" – taking off, landing, and even performing acrobatics.

Bud and other innovators even found ways to control the engine's speed with the use of insulated lines, a 9-volt battery pack, and electric relays hooked to the engine carburetors. Thus, you could land and take off many times in one flight. One of Bud's best achievements in 1946 was building a scale model DC-3 (two engine airliner) with a wingspan of six feet. This plane had the throttle controls previously mentioned. In flying the DC-3, it would take two or three laps around the pilot or controller to build up enough speed for takeoff. If one engine would quit running during flight, it would keep flying – barely.

In 1947 and 1948, Bud befriended several pilots through mutual businesses and by just visiting small airports in the Denver area. He was thus able to keep up his flying abilities, often just for buying gasoline for friends' airplanes. In 1948, Bud met a man who owned Denver Auto Electric Company in Englewood, Colorado. His name was Fred Cimzar, and he owned a 1947 Stinson Voyager Light four-passenger plane, powered by a 150 horsepower Lycoming engine. They became good friends and flew together for more than 25 years. Fred had his airplane tied down at Federal Heights Airport at 100th and Federal Boulevard. This was also the home of the "Flight Deck Lounge," a restaurant and bar adjacent to and owned by the airport manager. There was a flight school and planes to fly for rent on the field. Bud would often rent a J-3 Piper Cub and take me up for an hour ride. We would parallel Federal Boulevard when coming in to land, and the cars were going faster than we were. Cars were going 45-50 miles per hour, while the Cub was going 40 miles per hour.

Flying at Federal Heights at this time was limited to daylight hours, as there were no runway or other lights to light up the dark, dirt runway. Bud and two other pilots remembered Ray Wilson's Park Hill Airport, which had been closed for several years and was abandoned. This airfield had some small runway lights. On a Saturday these three men rented a small Ford tractor with an attached backhoe and dug up, transported, and reinserted the runway lights at Federal Heights. Soon after that, I remember getting a ride in the Stinson over Lakeside and Elitch Gardens Amusement Parks to see their pretty lights.

In 1953 Bud joined the Civil Air Patrol, which is an auxiliary of the United States Air Force. Bud was in Colorado Group 2 stationed at Lowry Air Force Base in Denver. In 1954 he was promoted to first lieutenant, and in 1957 he obtained his pilot rating, which enabled him to pilot USAF CAP planes. During this year, Bud spotted a tired, abandoned, three-seat Piper Cub Cruiser sitting in a corner of Federal Heights Airport. Upon inquiry, he found out the bridge builder for the Boulder Turnpike (U.S. 36) owned the plane. When the owner had finished his work on the highway in 1952, he left the airplane and returned to his home in the Midwest. Bud was able to purchase the aircraft for a small price, as it needed complete restoration and a new engine. Since Bud now had his own painting and decorating business, he could afford time and money to go on missions for the CAP and work on his own airplane. He rented hangar space at the small Englewood airport. There he put in a new cabin interior and recovered the entire airplane with new fabric. He then purchased a new 150 horsepower Super Cub engine from Lycoming.

By 1959, Bud had a rank of major with the Civil Air Patrol and was also appointed the Wing Flying Safety officer. The Englewood airport was closing in June of 1959 as land developers were going to start building houses there soon. Bud was frantically putting the finishing touches on his Cub Cruiser. I was volunteered to wax the fresh dope-covered fabric in late June, and Bud then test hopped the airplane. As he took off the runway, his plane was the last to leave Englewood Airport.

With his own airplane available, Bud could take off for CAP searches for missing or downed aircraft on short notice whenever needed, as he was his own boss. In June 1959, Bud received a Distinguished Service Award from the Civil Air Patrol "for Extraordinary Heroism while participating in a Civil Air Patrol Mission on 19 May 1959."

Flying over the Rocky Mountain front range on missing aircraft searches was often hazardous in small, light aircraft, as there were sometimes high winds coming over the mountain tops. Bud experienced these winds on a winter day search in 1958, when the air was very clear, but the westerly winds were apparently very strong. He came across the top of Rollins Pass flying west to east at 16,000 feet, which was about as high as his Cub Cruiser could go. Suddenly, a violent gust of wind and downdraft flipped his Cub over so that he was inverted and headed down in a dive. Fortunately, he had sufficient altitude and time to recover and head out east – at an airspeed of over 160 knots – with no added power of his engine. Bud always said, "You can't have too much altitude over the mountains" – even though the peaks where Bud went over the pass were only 12,000 to 13,000 feet high.

Bud went on many aerial searches for the Civil Air Patrol, both in his airplane or in Air Force L-16s or PA-18s. One time in 1959, Bud was with Paul Zeller, who was piloting the CAP Piper PA-18. They took off from Lowry Field on a training flight. Not far from Lowry, they looked down and observed an Air Force T-28 trainer that had made a forced landing in a plowed field and had flipped upside down. The pilots were apparently still inside the airplane. Fearing they might be trapped or their aircraft might catch fire, Bud and Paul made a quick decision to land and see if they could be of assistance. The CAP Cub was capable of landing in rough fields, so they felt a landing in the plowed field was safe. However, in his hurry to land, Paul misjudged his airspeed, stalled the airplane, and hit the ground, wingtip first and then the nose and engine. Both Paul and Bud were knocked unconscious. Paul died of his injuries, and Bud had a broken arm and unknown head and eye injuries. Ironically, the two T-28 pilots were not injured and called for a rescue helicopter from Lowry Field on their aircraft radio. Bud seemed to recover from his injuries rapidly and went back to flying within a few months.

Federal Heights Airport went the way of all the small airports in the Denver area in 1969, and it was closed by a real estate developer to build houses. Bud moved his airplane to Columbine Airport (which later became East Colfax Apartments) located on East Colfax (U.S. Highway 40) near Watkins, Colorado. Bud and three other pilots constructed a small hangar for their airplanes on that field.

Bud continued to fly for pleasure and on missions for the CAP through the early 1970s. In 1974, his eyesight started to fail to the extent that he could no longer fly. Apparently, his previous crash had damaged his vision irreversibly, and he was slowly going blind. Bud sold and delivered his Cub Cruiser to a pilot in Minnesota in 1974. He was able to fly in some friends' airplanes until 1975, but by 1975 he was back to constructing and flying model airplanes. He built several airplanes for his brother, me (his nephew), and even one of my children. Around this time, he retired from the Civil Air Patrol with the rank of lieutenant colonel. For the next 18 years his eyesight failed to the point where he was legally blind. He died in 2001 and left behind his love for aviation with many family members. During his lifetime, he built and flew more than 100 model airplanes. After his death, twenty of those planes went to an airplane museum in Northern California, and I inherited the rest of them.

Chapter 7

Bill Durlin, the third son of the Durlin family, was born in May of 1926. Even though he grew up in the shadow of Harry and Bob, he had more of a desire to learn and work on airplanes. In fact, everything mechanical interested him. With his older brothers already in the war in 1943, he wanted to do his part, and the Merchant Marine would take him at age 17. After serving in both the Pacific and Atlantic for two years, he came home in 1945.

He enrolled at Denver Opportunity School to learn aircraft mechanics. Unfortunately, his schooling was cut short with a draft notice from the Army. Bud advised Bill to tell his enlistment officer that he would like to take aircraft mechanic training. Probably because the war was almost over, the Army did grant his career wish. As a result, Bill served until early 1947 learning the aircraft mechanic trade.

Upon his military discharge, Bill was hired by Monarch Airlines in aircraft maintenance. Soon Monarch and Challenger Airlines merged to form Frontier Airlines. Bill worked his way up at Frontier, eventually becoming vice president in charge of engineering, even though he didn't have a college degree. When Frontier went out of business, he served Hawaiian Airlines as vice president and later worked for United Airlines before retiring.

But in 1993, an entrepreneur by the name of Sam Addoms called him. Sam wanted Bill to join him in starting a new Frontier Airlines. Sam, Bill, and nine other former airline executives met, and after a year they were able to get the new Frontier off the ground. Bill told Sam he would only work until he acquired six or seven airplanes for the new airline, as he was ready to retire at 67 years old. But Bill loved working in the airline industry so much that he didn't really retire until 2001, after acquiring thirteen good 737s for the airline.

Bill then devoted the rest of his life to traveling with his wife and doting over four children, thirteen grandchildren, twenty-one great-grandchildren, and two great-great-grandchildren. Bill died at sea between Greenland and Iceland while on a cruise in 2008.

Once, while Bill was working for Frontier Airlines, he had many of his younger staff over to the Wings Over the Rockies Museum for some meeting or event. His people were lined up in front of several of the vintage aircraft, and Bill glanced over his shoulder and spotted the Douglas B-18 bomber. He calmly said to his staff, "I worked on that plane."

All of them said, "We don't believe you – you're not that old and that plane probably wasn't even near you."

Actually, Bill had worked on the engines of that airplane at Denver Opportunity School in aircraft mechanic training.

Chapter 8

Gene Durlin was the youngster of the family, born in 1931. In his younger years he was mostly interested in drawing airplanes and reading about the latest types – especially during World War II. Being only eight years older than me, he taught me many things about airplanes, especially how to draw many types of airplanes. This training started when I was 4 years old and continued until my teens.

Gene graduated from high school in 1948 and soon joined the Air Force. After basic training he was sent to Eglin Air Force Base, Florida, to work in their photography lab. Eglin was, and still is, an Air Force Test Center for many facets of aircraft development and testing. After a two-year enlistment, Gene returned to Denver. But being in Air Force Reserve, when the Korean Conflict started, Gene was called back to active duty and returned to his old assignment at Eglin Field,

Florida. In 1953, when the Korean Conflict was over, he was discharged for good this time.

Epilogue

I was fortunate to grow up among several aviation lovers who passed the trait on to me. When I graduated high school and went to college, I was already hoping to fly in the military. I knew I couldn't be a pilot as I wore glasses, but I figured I could be a navigator or radar observer. I was "gung-ho" in Air Force ROTC, but I could not pass the flight physical. Everything was fine until they found me to be "shade confused" – a mild form of color blindness. Thus, for the rest of my life, I have been satisfied to be only an aviation fan. Denver has had an abundance of aviation pioneers, and also many ordinary people whose love of flying has enriched our local history. My family was a part of this history from the 1930s through the 1970s. Because of the efforts of the Wings Over the Rockies Air & Space Museum, this colorful Colorado history, and the broader national history of aviation, are still alive.

Bud Wolff on his 1918 Harley Davidson motorcycle in 1938.

Bud and Marge in front of his airplane, which he built with Marge's brothers in the Durlin family's basement.

Harry Durlin at Combs Field in Denver in 1942.

In 1943, Harry trained at Fort Stockton, Texas, in the Fairchild PT-19A.

HIGH ABOVE THE CITY - FOSTER FIELD, TEXAS.

Bob Durlin did his advanced training at Foster Field in 1942.

Bob in the cockpit of his P-47 at Bodney, Norfolk, in England, 1943.

BT-13s over the Colorado Rockies in 1944.

In 1945, Harry was a flight instructor at Page Field in Florida.

Harry with the first P-80A in Germany at Kitzingen AFB.

Two P-80s taking off at Kitzingen AFB in Germany, 1946.

The Durlin brothers in 1946. From left to right: Gene, Bill, Harry, and Bob.

Harry's very own F-80B "Maneuvers" at Ladd Field AFB in Alaska, 1948.

Harry stands in front of a F-80B at March Field in California, where he served with the 71st Fighter Squadron.

Harry getting ready for a mission in his F-86E at Suwon AFB in 1952.

MIG KILLER — Capt. Harry L. Durlin, was credited recently with damaging a Russian-built MIG 15 in a dogfight over Korea.

Clipping from a New Mexico newspaper in August, 1952.

Federal Heights Airport, 1952.

Bud's Cub Cruiser ready for its maiden flight at Englewood Airport, 1959.

Bud's Cub
Cruiser at
Federal
Heights
Airport,
1959.

Bud constructed this model DC-3 in 1946.

Bud with his scale models of the Staggerwing Beech and de Havilland Gypsy Moth airplanes in 1976. Bud constructed these using original plans of the full-scale airplanes.

Some notable pilots Harry knew, some were friends:

Buddy Bates – Primary, basic, advanced training, and Goodfellow Field

Charlie Francis – Fort Meyers, Sarasota, and Korea

Captain George Davis – 71st Fighter Squadron California, awarded Medal of Honor posthumously – 4th Fighter Group Korea

Major George Gleason – 71st Fighter Squadron and 36th Fighter Group Germany

Captain Don Adams – Kitzingen, Germany and 51st Fighter Group Korea

Captain-Lieutenant Colonel R. Creighton – 71st Fighter Squadron California and 51st Fighter Group Korea

Lieutenant Rex Taliaferro – Williams AFB Arizona and 71st Fighter Squadron California

Major Kincaid – 71st Fighter Squadron California

Captain Harry Evans – 36th Fighter Group Germany

*Captain Vince Gordon – 36th Fighter Group Germany

*Lieutenant Bill Patillo – 36th Fighter Group Germany

*Lieutenant Buck Patillo – 36th Fighter Group Germany

Major Walt Williams – 120th Squadron Colorado Air National Guard – Buckley Field and 51st Fighter Group Korea (He later was General Williams and commanded the 140th wing of the Colorado Air National Guard.)

Paddy Harbison – RAF exchange pilot with the 71st Fighter Squadron California

Major Hern – 36th Fighter Group Germany

Colonel "Gabby" Gabreski – group commander of the 51st Fighter Group Korea

*These were three of the original members of the first Air Force Aerobatic team that began in 1949. This team later evolved into the first USAF Thunderbirds aerobatic team.

Aviation acquaintances and pilot friends of Bud:

Dick Wood – painting boss and later pilot

Fred Cimzar – pilot

Ray Wilson – flight instructor, pilot, Bud's best man in his wedding and founder of Frontier Airlines

Frank Vandersarl – early aviation pioneer who sold Bud his first airplane in pieces

Lloyd Munson – pilot and friend

Frank Woodmansee – pilot

Trueman Wood "Woody" – pilot